D0065880

SECRETS FOR

WOMEN

J. Donald Walters

Hardbound edition, first printing 1993

Copyright 1993
J. Donald Walters

Illustrations copyright 1993
Crystal Clarity, Publishers

ISBN 1-56589-036-1

PRINTED IN HONG KONG

Crystal *Clarity*
P U B L I S H E R S

14618 Tyler Foote Road, Nevada City, CA 95959
1 (800) 424-1055

A SEED THOUGHT IS OFFERED FOR EVERY DAY OF THE MONTH. BEGIN A DAY AT THE APPROPRIATE DATE. REPEAT THE SAYING SEVERAL TIMES: FIRST OUT LOUD, THEN SOFTLY, THEN IN A WHISPER, AND THEN ONLY MENTALLY. WITH EACH REPETITION, ALLOW THE WORDS TO BECOME ABSORBED EVER MORE DEEPLY INTO YOUR SUBCONSCIOUS. THUS, GRADUALLY, YOU WILL ACQUIRE A COMPLETE UNDERSTANDING OF EACH DAY'S THOUGHT. AT THIS POINT, INDEED, THE TRUTHS SET FORTH HERE WILL HAVE BECOME YOUR OWN.

KEEP THE BOOK OPEN AT THE PERTINENT PAGE THROUGHOUT THE DAY. REFER TO IT OCCASIONALLY DURING MOMENTS OF LEISURE. RELATE THE SAYING AS OFTEN AS POSSIBLE TO REAL SITUATIONS IN YOUR LIFE.

THEN AT NIGHT, BEFORE YOU GO TO BED, REPEAT THE THOUGHT SEVERAL TIMES MORE. WHILE FALLING ASLEEP, CARRY THE WORDS INTO YOUR SUBCONSCIOUS, ABSORBING THEIR POSITIVE INFLUENCE INTO YOUR WHOLE BEING. LET IT BECOME THEREBY AN INTEGRAL PART OF YOUR NORMAL CONSCIOUSNESS.

Be true to yourself, and less concerned with what others think of you. Don't accept their definitions of you, but grow into a self-identification of your own.

Give from your own strength. Depend less on the strengths of others. Develop your own talents, and don't envy other people theirs.

A vortex of disturbed emotions is often dissipated by a sense of humor, and a heartfelt laugh.

Day Four

Transcend your personal troubles by offering solace to other troubled hearts.

Day 5

The
greatest
of
all
healers
is
love.

Day Six

Deepen your receptivity, that you receive on every level of your being the experiences in your life. Let them gestate silently. Then offer them back in the form of wisdom and new life for others.

Day Seven

Let your smiles be conceived in your heart, and given birth in the world through your eyes. Let your smiles be smiles of friendship, healing, and appreciation.

Don't concentrate on drawing others by your beauty, or by your feminine magnetism. For though it may be satisfying, at first, to find that you have this power over others, you will find it self-diminishing in time. Seek self-expansion, rather, by inspiring people; by appealing to the highest that is in them.

When

DAY NINE

TEMPTED TO UTTER CAUSTIC OR SARCASTIC REMARKS, REFLECT THAT AN EXCESS OF PEPPER CAN SPOIL A GOOD MEAL. HASTY WORDS HAVE RUINED MANY A PRECIOUS FRIENDSHIP, BUT NOTHING IS EVER LOST BY KINDNESS. GIVE OTHERS THE FREEDOM TO GROW AT THEIR OWN PACE.

Day Ten

EXPAND

your capacity for loving

into impersonal love for

all humanity, for all life.

Nurture others,

and in the nurturing you yourself will be

nourished, from within. A wise man once

said, "The channel is blessed by that

which flows through it."

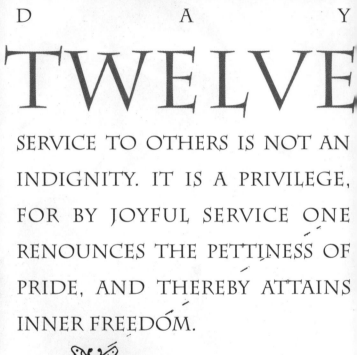

D   A   Y

TWELVE

SERVICE TO OTHERS IS NOT AN
INDIGNITY. IT IS A PRIVILEGE,
FOR BY JOYFUL SERVICE ONE
RENOUNCES THE PETTINESS OF
PRIDE, AND THEREBY ATTAINS
INNER FREEDOM.

Day Thirteen

Whenever we belittle others, we expose to them our own insecurity. Graciousness to all is the echo of inner victories.

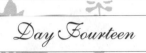

Day Fourteen

To overcome a tendency to take things too personally, refer what you hear from others to impersonal principles.

Day Fifteen

What we affirm in our hearts determines what we become. If we concentrate on littleness, we ourselves become petty. But if we concentrate on high thoughts and high ideals, we ourselves achieve greatness.

Day Sixteen

The way we look at life is colored by our feelings. A negative mood can make even white look gray. A positive mood can make even a gray day beautiful. Rely less on moods. Let your feelings be impartial; keep them centered in inner calmness.

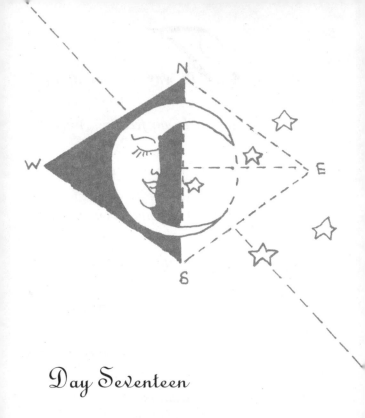

Day Seventeen

Women

are often highly intuitive, when their

feelings are calm, and grounded in

receptivity. Intuition _is_ calm, receptive

feeling.

CONCENTRATE MORE
ON THE LONGER RHYTHMS
IN YOUR LIFE. DWELL LESS
ON THE UPS AND DOWNS OF
THE MOMENT; MORE ON
PERMANENT REALITIES.

DAY EIGHTEEN

DAY NINETEEN

LET YOUR FEELINGS BE
GUIDED BY WISDOM, AND
YOUR EMOTIONS BY SELFLESS
LOVE.

ATHENA, GODDESS
OF WISDOM

Give of yourself impersonally, rather than thinking in terms of what others are giving you.

Day Twenty

True

Day Twenty-One

beauty

is a radiance outward from within. It comes from kind, happy thoughts, and from virtuous qualities. Beauty is not the outer mask a person wears to please the world. It is erroneous to make a cult of youth. Every age has its intrinsic beauty.

Day Twenty-Two

Show

your appreciation.
Show it more for the
giver than for the gift.

UNTRUTH HAS NO LASTING POWER.

IGNORE PEOPLE'S CRITICISMS, IF THEY ARE

WRONG, AND IF THEY ARE RIGHT, THANK

THEM (IF ONLY SILENTLY). DEFEAT

UNKINDNESS BY SPEAKING WELL OF THOSE

WHO ARE UNKIND TO YOU. THE BEST WAY

TO COMBAT DARKNESS IS NOT WITH AN

INCREASE OF DARKNESS, BUT WITH LIGHT.

LESSEN

your likes and dislikes. Find contentment

within yourself, and in the lasting blessing

of true friends.

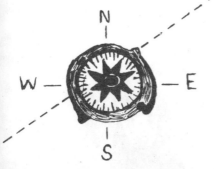

ct more; react less. Emotional reaction only clouds reality. Let your love for others be like a compass needle, which, no matter how often it is deflected, returns to the true North. Base your behavior on what you feel is right and true. Base it on what you believe will be of the greatest benefit to everyone.

Be concerned not with pleasing others, but with being a sincere friend to them.

Day Twenty-Six

Life can be, if you allow it, like a roller coaster ride: up one day, down the next. Act from your inner center. Whether things go well for you, or ill, reflect: All things must change. Don't get elated or depressed, for nothing in this universe will remain the same forever. Practice even-mindedness.

Day Twenty-Seven

Be fair. When

understand and respect their

understanding is there a hope of

is what counts, ultimately, not

♎

conversing with others, try to

points of view. For only by

changing anyone. Truth alone

opinions.

Be to everyone, in a sense, a mother. Give to others unconditionally; expect nothing in return. By so doing, you will receive from Life a thousandfold.

Day Thirty

*W*hen people hurt you,

heal their sickness of disharmony

by kindness, understanding,

and forgiveness.

Feminine

qualitities are as strong, in their own way, as those which are more distinctly masculine. Air and water are as powerful as fire. Patient endurance, receptivity, and the ability to adapt to circumstances ensures victory, often, where aggressiveness crashes in defeat.

Other Books in the **Secrets** Series
by J. Donald Walters

Secrets of Happiness

Secrets of Friendship

Secrets of Inner Peace

Secrets of Success

Secrets of Love

Secrets for Men

Coming Soon:

Secrets of Prosperity

Secrets of Leadership

Secrets of Self-Acceptance

Secrets of Winning People

Secrets of Radiant Health and Well-Being

Selected Other Titles
by J. Donald Walters

The Art of Supportive Leadership
(book, audio, video)
How to Spiritualize Your Marriage
Education for Life
Money Magnetism
The Path (the autobiography of J. Donald Walters)

Ask for these titles at your local bookstore.

For a free catalog of these books and other selections, please fill out the opposite side of this card, and send to Crystal Clarity, Publishers, 14618 Tyler Foote Road, Nevada City, CA 95959, or call 1-800-424-1055.

I just read _____
title of book

and loved it. I bought it at _____
name of store

in _____
city, state, zip

☐ Please send me your complete catalog of books, audios, and videos.

☐ Please add my name to your mailing list.

Name _____

Address _____

City _____ State ____ Zip _____

Phone _____
Daytime   Evening